INTO THE LIONS' PIT

Jennifer Rees Larcombe

Illustrated by Steve Björkman

Marshall Pickering
An Imprint of HarperCollins*Publishers*

Marshall Pickering is an Imprint of
HarperCollins*Religious*
Part of HarperCollins*Publishers*
77–85 Fulham Palace Road,
London W6 8JB
www.christian-publishing.co.uk

First published in 1992 in Great Britain
by Marshall Pickering as part of the
Children's Bible Story Book by Jennifer Rees Larcombe
This edition published in 2000 by Marshall Pickering

1 3 5 7 9 10 8 6 4 2

Text copyright © 1992, 2000 Jennifer Rees Larcombe
Illustrations copyright © 2000 Steve Björkman

Jennifer Rees Larcombe and Steve Björkman assert the moral right to be
identified as the author and illustrator of this work.

A catalogue record for this book is
available from the British Library.

ISBN 0 551 03248 0

Printed and bound in Hong Kong

INTO THE LIONS' PIT

Three men **crouched** in the bushes at the bottom of Daniel's garden.

'There he is,' they whispered, 'praying again!

We'll soon be **rid** of him now!'

Daniel knelt down by the open window of his bedroom.

Three times every day he prayed there as he looked out towards **Jerusalem**.

He did not care that a law had been passed in the land to say **no one was allowed to pray** for a whole month.

As he knelt there that day, praying for Jerusalem, he tried to remember how it had looked. It was **so many years** since he had been there, and tears began to run down his cheeks.

'**Please** God, forgive your people the Jews,' he sobbed. 'We are so **sorry** we turned away from you.

Please let us go back and rebuild our land.'

Just then a wonderful thing happened.

The angel Gabriel himself suddenly appeared beside him, but only Daniel knew he was there.

'God loves you,' he said, 'and He hears your prayer. Soon Jerusalem will be rebuilt, and not long after that God will send His Messiah.

But when men **kill him** unfairly,
Jerusalem will have to be destroyed once again.'

Daniel **bowed** his head and thought
about this **strange message**,
but he never realized his enemies
were still watching him.

The new King Darius **liked** Daniel
very much and he had made
him very important again.

That made other men so **jealous**,
they began looking out for ways
to get Daniel **into trouble**.

'You are so great,' they said to the King, 'you should show everyone you are as powerful as any god. Make a rule that no one prays except to you for a whole month. If they do, have them thrown into a pit of hungry lions.'

The King felt **most flattered**, but he did not realize they were only trying to **trap** their enemy.

They knew Daniel would take no notice of this rule and would **go on praying** three times a day, just like he **always** had.

'We've got you now!' they **sniggered** from their hiding place in the garden.

'Let's go and tell the King!'

Darius was terribly upset.

'**However** will I manage without Daniel?' he wondered. All day long he tried to think of a way of saving his friend, but Persian laws could **never** be changed, not even by the King.

So, in the evening, soldiers came and **threw** Daniel down into the pit of lions.
'May your God keep you safe!' shouted the King as he watched Daniel **disappear.**

Sadly he trailed home to his palace and went to bed without **any** supper.

All night long he **tossed and turned**, worrying about poor Daniel. Could his God save him? He had once saved those three men in the fire, but he shook his head sadly when he thought about those

fierce lions.

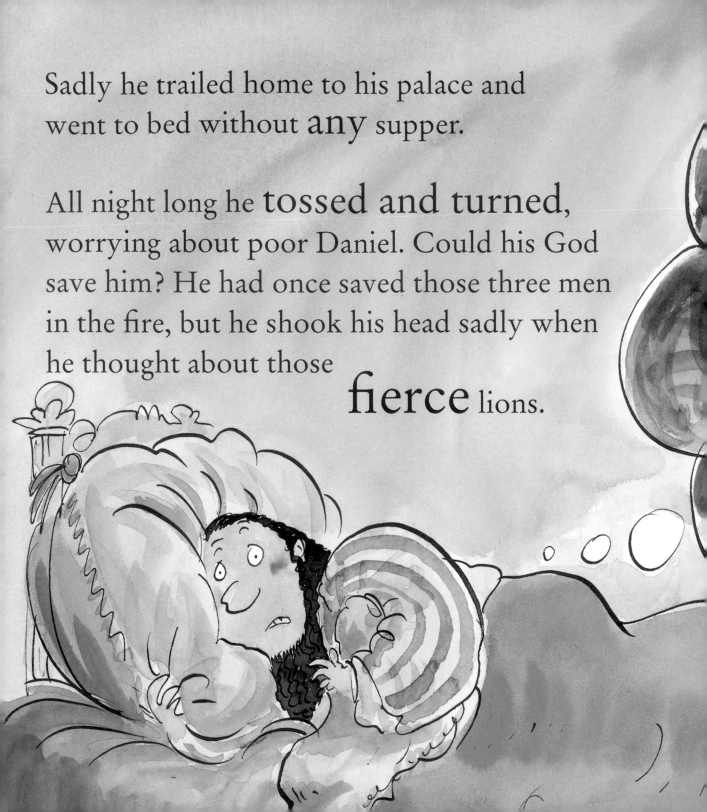

As soon as it was light, he hurried to the lions' pit and had the heavy, stone door moved away.

'Daniel,' he called,

'has your God saved you?'

'Yes, your Majesty,' came Daniel's voice from far below.

'His angel shut the mouths of the lions.'

Darius was so delighted he had Daniel pulled out at once and his enemies were thrown into the pit instead.

The lions tore them to pieces before they even reached the ground!

From that day King Darius

believed in God

for the rest of his life.

Daniel 9, 6